How To Save Money, Stay On A Budget And Get Out Of Debt.

Joe Rovito

This book is presented solely for educational and entertainment purposes. The author and publisher are not offering it as legal, accounting, or other professional services advice. While best efforts have been used in preparing this book, the author and publisher make no representations or warranties of any kind and assume no liabilities of any kind with respect to the accuracy or completeness of the contents and specifically disclaim any implied warranties of merchantability or fitness of use for a particular purpose. Neither the author nor the publisher shall be held liable or responsible to any person or entity with respect to any loss or incidental or consequential damages caused, or alleged to have been caused, directly or indirectly, by the information or programs contained herein. No warranty may be created or extended by sales representatives or written sales materials. Every company is different and the advice and strategies contained herein may not be suitable for your situation. You should seek the services of a competent professional before beginning any improvement program. The story and its characters and entities are fictional. Any likeness to actual persons, either living or dead, is strictly coincidental.

Table of Contents

Chapter 1 - The Start Of How It All Begin - Yes It Can Be Done

Chapter 2 - Credit Score - How to raise your credit score in a few simple steps.

Chapter 3 - Credit Score - Reasons to have a high credit score.

Chapter 4 - APR - Annual Percentage Rate:

Chapter 5 - Budget - Why make a budget:

Chapter 6 - Mortgage Pay Off - Why pay more towards your mortgage?

Chapter 7 - Strategy For Getting Out Of Debt - What works to get out of debt

Chapter 8 - Steps To Pay Off Debt - Is There Really A System?

Chapter 9 - Debt Consolidation - Why you should not do it!

Chapter 10 - Raise Your Income - Getting Out Of Debt Quicker.

Chapter 11 - Taxes - Saves You A Lot If You Do Them Right!

Chapter 12 - Coupons - Save Money Tax-Free

Conclusion

Chapter 1

The Start Of How It All Begin - Yes It Can Be Done

My story of how I got out of debt is a fairly quick one. I was about 20 years old and open my first credit card. I charged about 20 bucks on it. Then, I got my first bill. $23.00 dollars!?!? Could not believe it. I called the bank where I got the card from and immediately canceled the card. Made the payment and was done.

Then fast forward about 10 years. I am living at a friends house, paying about $400 in rent with all utilities included except my cable. Not a bad setup looking back. I had a little savings living there. I also had a bad gambling problem that would not let me get my head above water. I had to often borrow money for rent. I had no other bills at this time and made about $2700 a month. Somehow I had $0 dollars to my name.

I finally moved out of my buddies room ready to make the jump to living on my own. You definitely cannot do much with our cash or credit. Both of which I had none. I had no money to pay my rent, no couch, a mattress. I went gambling stressed on what little money I had trying to win more to pay my rent. Lost everything. I had to call my uncle to borrow $1000 to make rent. Then I went to a local furniture store to get a couch. I did not have bad credit, I had no credit which can be equally as bad. A score of about 550. I had to basically pay about $1000 for a $600 couch. I used the store's in-house credit department to build credit. It was called AcceptanceNow. The store was Becks Furniture. I recommend this store or any store that has this program if you are in a similar situation. They report directly to the credit bureau. All you have to do is make the minimum payment on time every month.

Now that I had furniture and rent paid, I worked on getting out of debt. Which was only $1600. Paid my uncle back and now all I have left is my couch. After making payments on my couch for 9 months, my score went up and decided to pay the remaining balance on my couch.
Step two I opened a credit card with my bank. Now opening a credit card is not the same as racking up a $1000 dollar on it. I made a $100 purchase and made monthly payments for about 4-5 years. I kept my balance at about $100 the whole time. Just in case I ran into trouble and had to use it.

I managed to save about $20,000 and a 750 credit score. I was living on my own, renting, working. Financed a car that I realized I needed to pay off.

Bam, $9263. Paid in full. I am now debt-free, except for my house. I borrowed $179,000 to buy it. If you compare renting to a mortgage payment then you quickly realize that you are only paying someone else mortgage or just fattening the pockets of that apartment complex. I wanted to stop that and made a choice to buy a home. I did not rush into it.

There was criteria that had to be met before I made the choice to put an offer on a home. 1. The neighborhood had to be good for the price. 2. I did not want to go over my monthly budget of $1500. 3. The home had to be big enough my girlfriend and I could enjoy it. All 3 of these items were met. There are a few tricks you can do to help pay down your mortgage. I will go over that in a later chapter. Paid off all my memberships, credit score is good now so I paid off my credit card. And now have $0 debt other than my house. There is nothing greater.

Chapter 2

Credit score - How to raise your credit score in a few simple steps.

When raising your credit score there are a few key factors.

1. Make on-time payments. The lender that is lending you money to buy whatever goods you want is looking at how consistent you make your payments.

2. Use a small percentage of the overall amount. For instance, if you are at $1000 credit limit use $50 bucks or so.

3. Do not close accounts unless you have to. Credit cards (unless there are fees involved) should not be closed. They can be left open. Store cards like Target or Walmart cards can be left open as long as there are no fees involved. Just cut them up and act like you never had them. After they are paid in full. When paying off your car, you can possibly affect your credit. It closes the account with the lender. Closed accounts hurt.

4. Time, it takes time to raise your score. Took me a few years to get to 750. Be patient.

Chapter 3

Credit score - Reasons to have a high credit score.

Some reasons to have a great credit score is making big purchases. Like buying a house, the better the credit score the more programs you qualify for. Grants that you don't have to pay back. Or grants that do not have to be paid right away. You get a better rate. Other than your house you shouldn't need to use credit to pay for it. Pay cash!

This is a very short chapter. The answer is simple. Do not do it!

This brings me to my next section. APR.

Chapter 4

APR - Annual Percentage Rate:

This is huge if you do not understand how APR works. Let's say the bank loans you $1 at 17%. That means for each dollar you borrow the bank wants $.17 cents. Not bad if you only borrow a buck. Let's add a couple zeros on to the end of it. $1000 at 17% is $170 accrued in interest, every month.

For me, I like to keep my interest money and use it for other things. I am guessing you can see now why borrowing money and having an interest rate is a bad idea. If you think you are getting miles or gas points or some other item when you use your card, I am sure it comes at a price. Nothing is free.

Chapter 5

Budget - Why make a budget:

A budget is one of the best ways to help get out of debt and stay out of debt. What I do is simply write down all of my monthly bills. Mortgage, Insurance, Phone, Water etc... Then put a number by it. This is a simple way to know what's going out.

After you write down your monthly bills, add them up. Then add up 4 weeks of pay after tax. For instance, total bills equal $1000 subtracted by monthly income $2500 and you get $1500 left over. Then make a column for food and gas. Let's say $150 a week. $150 x 4 = $600. Now $1500 - $600 is $1100. To put towards bills or retirement or whatever you want. Here is an example budget I use.

Example Budget
Mortgage - $657
Insurance - $176
HOA - $120
Water - $40
Phone - $60
PG&E - $20
Smud - $75
Cable - $20

Total Monthly Bills - $1168.00

Monthly Income - $3200.00

Total Bills - Income = $2032.00

$1168 - $3200 = $2032

Non-Bill Monthly Expenses
Gas - $100
Food - $300
Savings - $800

Take the money left over from the Income - Total Bills and subtract non-bill monthly expenses total.

$100 + $300 + $800 = $1200.
$1200 - $2032 = $832. I have $832 to spend on anything I want. But we are going to throw it at our home. That brings me into the next chapter.

Chapter 6

Mortgage Pay Off - Why pay more towards your mortgage?

When it comes to paying off your mortgage there are tons of reasons to do it. The number one reason to pay more on your mortgage is to possibly shave off years on your 30 year fixed loan. If there are no fees by your mortgage company that is. Looking at my breakdown on my mortgage bill I have 3 different areas that I am paying.

1. Principal - $201.08

2. Interest - $803.79

3. Escrow (Taxes & Insurance) $308.92.

If you haven't noticed the issue here then I will point it out to you. It is that I am paying $803.79 in interest. This is pretty insane. By paying an extra $200 dollars a month towards principal, you knock off years of paying your mortgage.

$200 x 12 = $2400. That is an extra couple of payments maid which brings down your balance. Now if you don't have an extra $200 a month than throw whatever money you can at it. Even if it is only $25.

This is also a nice time to say not to get into too much payment for your home. If you have a payment of $2500 a month and that maxes you out then you cannot throw more money at the principal. If you make the minimum payments for 30 years you will end up paying double for your home. For instance, a $150,000 house will cost you roughly $300,000. $300,000 will cost you $600,000. These are not exact numbers. But I am sure you are getting the picture. You will actually pay more than double over the entire life of the loan on a 30 year fixed making monthly minimum payments.

Chapter 7

Strategy For Getting Out Of Debt - What works to get out of debt and save money

When it comes to a strategy to getting out of debt there are a few ways to tackle it. The first one I like to do when looking to save money, it's a little something I call "Trim The Fat". This means going down your monthly bill list to see what you can shave off.

Cable/Internet, we were paying $65 - $90 a month for cable and internet. I called the cable company and asked what other plans they have. Since I rarely watch cable I asked for internet only. $40 bucks a month plus tax is about $43.29 split with my girlfriend and I pay $21.65 a month for high speed internet. We do stream Netflix and Prime on my XBox for entertainment.

Phone, Plans are a perfect way to shave some money. I had to pay a monthly payment for my phone, (I think most phone companies do this now). It is $17.00 a month plus our plan totaling about $60. This is something that I have been doing for a long time. I adjust my plan to be as minimal as possible and still have reliable service. I use my WIFI to cover data when at home.

Insurance, yes, another way to save some money! My insurance was at $245 a month, crazy I know. Super expensive. Paid off my car, shopped around using Cost U Less insurance (insurance broker) and found a deal for $176. The catch to this is you have to pay $300 or so up front and it included my first 20 days of insurance.

This is another no-brainer if you look at the savings each month. $245 - $176 = $69 a month savings. $69 x 12 = $828 in savings a year. So you can see why I really like this one! You do have to pay attention to coverage which is a huge factor. I still have full coverage and a $1000 deductible. Instead of $500. But if you look at the savings the first year you see that this pays for itself even after the deductible if needed.

Utilities, a couple ways to save here. One is based on income. You can call your local utility company and see if you qualify for any programs that can help with the monthly bill. Another way to save is by reducing your heating and air bill.

If you can research Items to keep the sun out in the summer and the heat in, in the winter. Now one season is probably worse than the other. Here in Sacramento where I live, summer is a bear and winter is manageable. So our bill in the winter will be less since we can dress warmer. In places like Colorado, it might be in reverse.

Car, why buy a car and pay extra money when you can save up and pay cash. This makes total sense if you think about it. You pay an additional $1000 - $5000 or more depending on your interest rate. Why not save up, pay cash and put that interest back into your pocket.
Go through your monthly bills and see what one you can trim. You might save a bit of money each year.

Overall there are many things you can do on a monthly basis to save money.

Here are a few more tips about saving money. Call your local utility company and see if they offer any programs for single parents or limited income.

This can possibly cut your huge heating and cooling bill in half.

This might sound like a given, but wear a jacket in the winter and shorts in the summer. The most expensive time to run any appliance is from 4pm to 8pm.

This might very in your area. Point is to try and avoid peak times to run any appliances.

By a fan. Yes buying a fan will help cool your house a bit. You can try covering the windows to block out the heat. There are a few items on Amazon that are cost effective. They work amazing!

Chapter 8

Steps To Pay Off Debt - Is There Really A System?

Yes, yes, yes. A trick to this is either pay off the higher interest rate first. Or pay off your lowest owed amount first. For instance, if you have a credit card you owe $150 on at 17% it might be a good idea to knock that one out. If you have a Target card at $100 with 20% interest than you can probably want to pay that one off soon..

The overall goal is to pay one credit card or piece of debt at a time. If we have $250 dollars, we pay off both Target and credit card asap. If we do not have the money than we pay off one or the other and take the money we were paying monthly and apply it to another bill.

Here is an example of what some people might owe and how to go about paying the debt.

1. Subscription magazine 0%. Owed $145. Monthly minimum payment $26

2. Credit card 17% interest rate. Owed $350. Monthly minimum payment $27

3. Target card 20% interest rate. Owed $500. Monthly minimum payment $25

4. Phone 0% interest rate. Owed $700. Monthly minimum payment $26

If you look at the list above we see the list is in order of lowest to highest. A proven way to pay these debts off is to start with the lowest one fist. Bam!

Number 1, gone. Now take that $26 a month you were paying on the subscription and put it towards number.

2. That is $53 dollars a month going towards number 2. Pay that off, then take that $53 and put it towards number.

3. When doing these steps you start to feel accomplished and see a light at the end of the

tunnel. You will be paying the same amount monthly but in the most efficient way.

Chapter 9

Debt Consolidation - Why you should not do it!

There is no better way to waste your money than to pay a company a fee to help lower your debt. Think about it, I pay you a fee and you lower my monthly payments. Okay, cool. But How long do I have to pay on that? There is really nothing good about using debt consolidation. This will be a very short chapter. It is very simple, do not do it!

Instead, do the tips I mentioned previously about paying off debt and you will be home free in no time! This is one of the biggest mistakes you can do.

Chapter 10

Raise Your Income - Getting Out Of Debt Quicker.

One way to get out of debt is to raise your income. Get a new job, get a second job. Why settle for less if you're not making what you should be. This is one of the quickest ways to debt freedom, and one of the most well known. What is not well known is that when you increase your pay you more likely to increase your spending.

For instance, you get a raise and now you feel you need a new car, now your minus $500 a month or more. Now you want to buy a home and increase your monthly payment by let's say another $500. Instead of making an extra $1000 a month, you now make the exact same amount with some better things. Instead of banking or investing that $1000. The point I'm trying to make is that when you o increase your pay do not go beyond your means and get into even more debt.

Go back to school if that is what it will take to get a higher paying job. Or get a certification. This is an amazing time to be alive. Information is at your fingertips. All you have to do is try.

Chapter 11

Taxes - Saves You A Lot If You Do Them Right!

If you are like most Americans than you pay your taxes at the end of the year. Most Americans pay anywhere from 10% - 37% of your income to the government. There are few ways to help bring that percentage down.

One of them is to start a business. Now definitely be sure to check with your local tax person or state for there rules when filing income taxes. But one thing I learned from doing real estate is that the right offs are amazing!

If you have a room that you use as an office for work, that is a write-off, your mileage when meeting a client is a write-off, office supplies for your business is a write-off. If you buy clothes for your business or take a client out to a sporting event a portion of that can be used as a write-off. Give a housewarming gift, that is a write-off. If you pay association dues that can be a write-off. You can see that owning a company that makes you money can also save you money on things that would normally cost you if you worked for an employer.

Chapter 12

Coupons - Save Money Tax-Free

You may not realize it, but when you save money with coupons or buy items on sale you increase your profit for the year. For instance, if you by toothpaste and it normally is $3 and you buy it on sale for $1.50, this is an immediate saving that is not taxable. So that $1.50 goes directly back in your pocket on something that you would normally be buying anyway.

If you have a coupon for a free combo meal from a restaurant, but you would have to buy one to get it. Find someone to split the bill with and you both save a few bucks. Now instead of making $30,000.00 a year, you made $30,003.50. If you do this enough it will add up.

Chapter 13

Cut The Cord – Saving Money On Everyday Items

Why is it that people want to spend money on a $5 coffee? Then top it off with a $5.75 sandwich? That is a huge expense that you can cut right now and save that $10.75 a day.

Think about it, you can go to the local store, pick up a bag of coffee for $7. Buy a coffee maker for under $50. I use bottled water because it tastes better. Buy your favorite creamer for around $3 - $5.

Now other than the coffee maker your total for a weeks worth of coffee is about $11.

You save each day and use that money towards your credit card debt. Now, this is one item that is easy to cut back and save.

What other things can you do to save money?

How about rent a movie from Redbox instead of going out to the movies. If you do go to the movies, do not buy the popcorn and the soda.

Have some discipline until you get out of debt. Once your out of debt create a spoil me account. This account is only for fun stuff. Like trips, video games, appliances, furniture or whatever you want to spend your hard earned cash on.

Here is one tip that most do not know about saving money. It mainly applies to the people who own cars that use gas. Do not step on the gas so hard. You waste gas, then stop, then go, then stop. Be easy on the pedal and eliminate a few trips to the gas station over the year.

Drinking water when going out to eat might sound like an easy thing to do. Most do not like to do this. Something about a soda and a cheeseburger how they go hand and hand. What if I told you that it gets easier the more you replace soda with water. Then what if I told you sodas are one of the best ways for restaurants to make profit on.

Look at it like this, you buy a soda for lunch, no big deal. Let's say $1.99 + tax is about $2.14. Now on the other side of town your loved one is doing the same thing. Were at $4.28 for lunch sodas. $2.14 is actually cheap for a soda. Sometimes I see them for $2.99 or more.

Now it's dinner time, and you want another soda. $4.28 again. Bringing the total for soda cost to $8.56. By the time the work week is over you now spent $8.56 x 5 = $42.80 a week on soda. Take it one step further and do an average for the month $42.80 x 4 = $171.20.

You can see how something so small can add up really quickly. This is not counting weekends and the monthly total is coming close to about $200.

If you cut out soda for a 1 month you could easily pay down one of your credit cards or an extra couple hundred towards your car payment. If you do not have a spouse then cut the number in half. This is still a significant amount of money that could make a dent in your debt.

Chapter 14

Selling Unwanted Items – Amazon, Ebay Or Letgo

This is a simple way to sell used items for extra cash. My girlfriend loves shoes and has tons of them. When you went through her closet she found a few pairs that she no longer wears. Be it style, season, or doesn't fit. Whatever the case may be she has made a few bucks selling unwanted shoes. Some brands sell easier than others.

Kids items are also a great idea if your looking to make some extra cash. Think about it, kids grow out of clothes super fast. Why not capitalize on it and make some money. Our daughter had a few pairs of shoes she never wore and out grew. They sold in about 3 days.

Text books! Thats right, text books, fiction, non-fiction. They are very easy to sell on Amazon. All it takes is a few steps for you to start making some extra income off old books.

These items listed should not be the end all be all for you. Give it a try. Ebay doesn't charge to sell items until they actually sell. Then they charge a small percentage and take it from the seller.

One thing I like to point out when selling on Ebay is the shipping cost. Call your local post office and find out the amount to ship the item. Usually it is based off weight.

Finding items to sell on Ebay. I like ebay for a few reasons. Mainly, they make it extremely easy to use. And as mentioned above they are cheap and do not charge until the item sells.

When looking for items to sell online you can try a couple options. Check out your local Goodwill to see if anyone has donated any expensive items you can possibly resell. Check in more upscale neighborhoods for better items to sell. You can also try stores like Ross or Marshalls. These stores have items that resell on Ebay from a nice little profit if you do it well.

Checking misspelled words on Ebay or Letgo is a way to score on items that are just sitting. Sorry to say that capitalizing on others mistakes for a profit. If you do not, someone else will. For instance a bottle of alcohol was missed spelled and the seller lost out on over a million bucks. So it can pay to look up misspelled words like Diamonds, spelled Dimands.

Letgo is an easy way to sell items locally. I like this app for a few reasons also. Like selling bigger items such as BBQ, TV, furniture etc. They are also easy to sell and have a few options when accepting payments. One is accept payment first. My personal favorite since you really do not know who is buying your item.

Last but not least is.. you guessed it! Craigslist. That's right, this site is still one of the best places to sell an item. Craigslist gets millions of views every month. You still have to be careful when using this site. There has been some horror stories to be cautious and meet in public sites. Craigslist is also a good way to save on items. We bought out couch on Craigslist years ago and still using it till this day.

Chapter 15

Stop Spending Money - It's Easier Than You Think

One way to stop spending money is to understand why you spend money. One sales tactic company's use is to feed on your impulsive side.

You can also make a deal with yourself. Find something you like, wait a week to buy it. After that week of you still feel you want the item and you can justify it. Then you know it is something that is probably needed.

Another way to stop spending is to grocery shop and eat leftovers. If you can make a meal for $15 and it last 2 days for two people than that is only $3.75 a meal. Not a bad savings in the current world we live in. This was a hard thing for my girlfriend to do. Until she started to save money each week. Now she is on board with reheating leftovers and even wonders how food will taste the next day.

Another way to save money is price comparison. Shop around do not settle for one price until you have confirmed you cannot find it for cheaper.

You can also by the store brand on some items. Some items like local grocery stores to a good job at matching well known brands. If this saves money then it's definitely worth it.

Chapter 16

The Jones - How Buying Clothes Can Be Cheap

Buying clothes can come at unexpected times. You need to dress well for an interview. Or you got the job and now you need work clothes. A special occasion can come up and you need to update your wardrobe.

Buy on sale! It is better to buy clothes in the clearance section than rack up debt on that store credit card that charges you 20% interest. Take your time and look through carefully. You can even plan ahead if needed. By summer clothes when no one else wants them, in the winter. Or buy winter clothes in the summer.

My favorite store to shop at for sale item is Kohls. I can literally walk into a Kohl's men's clearance section and spend $20 and walk out with 5 shirts.

They have tons of items on clearance if they don't sell. For every week they are on sale and don't sell they drop in price. You can literally buy a shirt for $1 - $2. They also have more than one section of clearance.

If you need work out clothes check out Kohl's workout section and pick up shorts and a tank top for just a few bucks.

Sales, sometimes they happen. You might need to use your store card to get the sale. That is okay, use it to save an extra 20% - 30%. Here is the catch, you pay off the balance while you're still in the store. Just let the cashier know what you intend to do.

Cut monthly subscriptions - anything you can do for free like a music subscription cut it and save that $5.

Gym you can either find a new gym to go to or try and reduce your current membership. Some clubs have every other day membership that reduce the monthly cost.

My gym has memberships for just $10. That's it. And once a year they charge you a small fee of around $50. Now this is a large fee but averaged out it's an additional $4.16 a month. Your now at $14.16 a month. I know some people that pay $50 - $60 a month.

If you want to keep your gym and they won't reduce your membership, try to add a friend or family member to get a discount and split the monthly bill.

Ask your local gym what you can do to minimize your monthly bill but still keep the gym you like. Another way to choose a gym is pick up the phone and see who has the best deal at that time. I know a few gyms that run promotions and you can pick up a membership for most places for under $20.

I love the free weights at my gym, and the treadmill, but some don't like either. You can cancel that gym membership and pocket that extra $10 - $30 a month and throw it at some debt.

Chapter 17

Invest In Yourself - Pay #1

Save a percentage of your paycheck each month.

Now there is actually a way to do this. Believe it or not. You want to save up a small emergency fund. Around $1000. After that $1000 is saved you throw everything you have at debt. You budget monthly and throw everything you can at debt. Rinse and repeat.

Now if you are out of debt you are now able to throw 15% into retirement. When you get a raise you don't need to get a new car with the money. Instead, take the wage increase you just got and put it towards retirement.

Or what I like to do is start a small business. The reason why I do this is only for a few simple reasons. I can make more return on my money by investing in a business rather than my retirement. For instance, in a aggressive mutual fund you can make 8% - 17% ROI (Return on investment). You can also watch the money you invested disappear.

That's why I like affiliate marketing and running a blog that can potentially make a 500% ROI. I do lose a little time setting up the business at first and a few hours writing articles each week. If blogging is not your thing try starting an a E-Commerce store and do drop shipping.

You can also pick up a telecommuting position and work from home. That is 0 gas, 0 traffic and a part time gig to earn some extra retirement income.

If you do put the money into an account be careful, do your research on the pros and cons. If you're not careful where you put your money you can lose it all. 401K are a safe bet to build wealth over time. I also like roth 401K. This is a taxed 401K. What that means is that the money that goes in is taxes instead of when you take it out.

Now you may he wondering why you would do this. Well, it is actually quite simple. Do you think taxes will rise in the future?

I do. I am not 100% since we cannot predict the future. But I think that the tax rate will increase along with inflation on our dollar. This is just my opinion, check with a financial planner and don't be afraid to get a second opinion

If an employer matches you on a 401K up to a certain percentage. Do it. That money can cover most of the taxes that might be taken out later on in retirement.

There are tons of places to put your money, I recommend a great book by Tony Robbins called "Money Master The Game". Be sure to check it out. Everything you want to know as a beginner is in that book. I like the audio version.

Conclusion - And Or Questions

We were never taught how to not create debt in school. We were actually taught to go into debt. What is the next big thing, spend, spend, spend. If you picked up this digital book then that means you are taking the next step to happiness. You will feel like a weight is lifted off your shoulders. You can start to build real wealth for yourself when you're not paying interest or taxes to someone else.

I live what I preach, am happy to help in any way I can. If you have any questions about the book feel free to contact me at succorhacks@gmail.com. Trust me there is nothing better than spending your hard earned money on you and the ones you love. Buckle down and let's get debt free!!

www.ingramcontent.com/pod-product-compliance
Lightning Source LLC
Chambersburg PA
CBHW031556210526
45464CB00003B/1312